Meditation and Me

Written by William Anthony
Designed by Danielle Rippengill

©Published 2022.
BookLife Publishing Ltd.
King's Lynn, Norfolk PE30 4LS

ISBN 978-1-80155-155-7

All rights reserved. Printed in Poland.
A catalogue record for this book is available
from the British Library.

Meditation and Me
Written by William Anthony
Designed by Danielle Rippengill

An Introduction to Accessible Readers...

Our 'really readable' Accessible Readers have been specifically created to support the reading development of young readers with learning differences, such as dyslexia.

Our aim is to share our love of books with children, providing the same learning and developmental opportunities to every child.

INCREASED FONT SIZE AND SPACING improves readability and ensures text feels much less crowded.

OFF-WHITE BACKGROUNDS ON MATTE PAPER improves text contrast and avoids dazzling readers.

SIMPLIFIED PAGE LAYOUT reduces distractions and aids concentration.

CAREFULLY CRAFTED along guidelines set out in the British Dyslexia Association's Dyslexia-Friendly Style Guide.

Images courtesy of Shutterstock.com. Cover – Naoki Kim, tanyabosyk. 4 – iofoto. 5 – MintImages. 6 – Evgeny Atamanenko. 7 – SmartPhotoLab. 8 – Dmitry Kalinovsky. 9 – Africa Studio. 10 – kornnphoto. 11 – Quintanilla. 12 – Pixel-Shot. 13 – Comeback Images. 14 – wavebreakmedia. 15 – Suzanne Tucker. 16 – Creativa Images. 17 – Anatoliy Karlyuk. 18 – AnnGaysorn. 19 – Anukul. 20 – wavebreakmedia. 21 – jannoon028. 22 – Khosro. 23 – Desizned. 24 – wavebreakmedia. 25 – Amorn Suriyan. 26 – Monkey Business Images. 27 – KlingSup. 28 – Yuriy Mazur. 29 – Khosro.

Contents

Page 4 Healthy You

Page 6 What Is Meditation?

Page 8 Where Did Meditation Come From?

Page 10 Why Should I Meditate?

Page 14 Types of Meditation

Page 16 Mindfulness Meditation

Page 18 Focused Meditation

Page 20 Guided Meditation

Page 22 Yoga Meditation

Page 24 Where Can I Meditate?

Page 26 Looking After You

Page 30 Index

Page 31 Meditation: Quiz

Healthy You

Keeping your body healthy can mean lots of different things. It can mean eating healthy food, exercising, and resting well.

One of the most important parts of staying healthy is taking care of your mind.

Your mind is the part of you that thinks. It feels emotions and remembers things.

Having a healthy mind can help us in lots of ways. It may help us to think clearly, make better decisions and live better lives.

What Is Meditation?

Meditation is something useful that can help you to understand your thoughts and feelings. It can be difficult to learn. However, it can be very helpful when you get the hang of it!

People may meditate for lots of different reasons.

Some people may do it to relax and get rid of stress. Other people may do it to focus on the thoughts they have.

Where Did Meditation Come From?

We still don't really know where meditation came from. We also cannot even be sure who used it first or how old it is.

Some people believe it started thousands of years ago in India.

Today, millions of people from all around the world meditate.

People might meditate in a big class or at home on their own. Joining a class is a good way to find out if meditation is right for you.

Why Should I Meditate?

Meditation can help you in lots of ways. It can help you to focus and clear your mind when you have lots to think about. You can meditate whenever and wherever you feel comfortable.

Some people think that meditating often can help you to sleep better. Getting good sleep helps you feel healthy and full of energy.

Some people also believe that meditation may even help your body to be fitter and stronger.

Many artists meditate to help them come up with ideas.

Painters may meditate to picture a place or thing they wish to paint.

People who write songs may meditate to help them come up with lyrics.

Meditation isn't just for artists either. Lots of people who play sports meditate too. They can use it to help them prepare for a match. It can also help their body and mind recover after a match.

Types of Meditation

There are many different types of meditation. Different types of meditation can do different things for both your mind and your body. Some types of meditation involve sitting down with your eyes closed.

Some types of meditation are about giving all your attention to one thing. For example, in walking meditation you will focus on each step you take.

Other types of meditation are about clearing your mind and not focusing on anything!

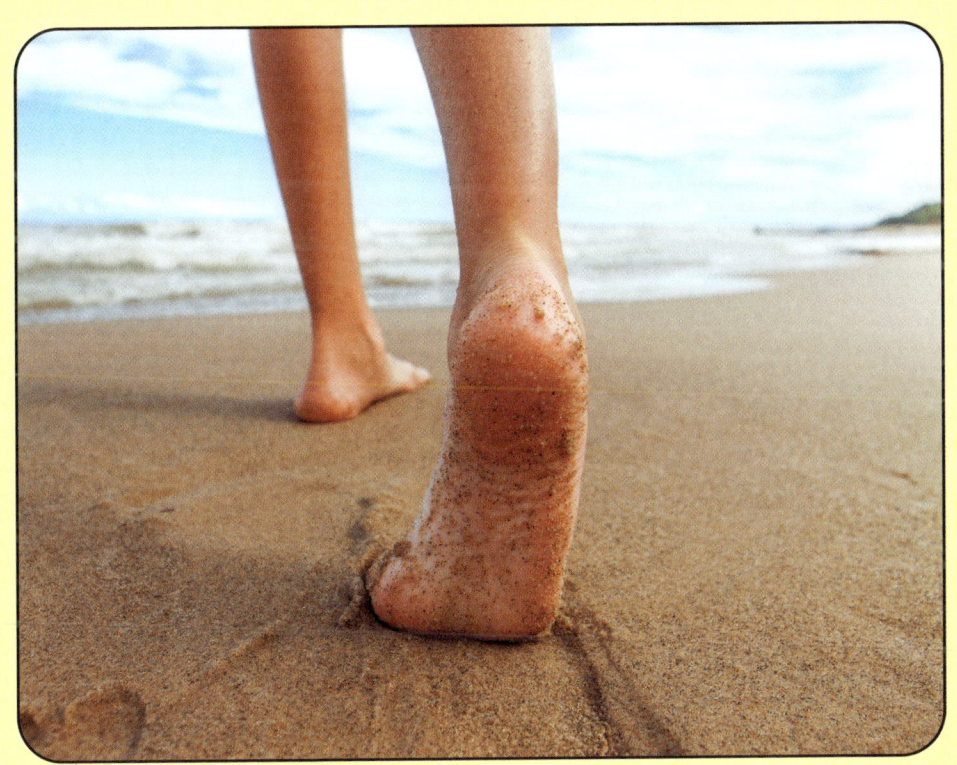

Mindfulness Meditation

Mindfulness meditation is about noticing what is happening around you and what you are thinking. Don't focus on any one thing. If a thought comes into your head, just notice it and let it move on.

In mindfulness meditation, we would only notice that we were waiting in a queue, rather than get annoyed at having to wait.

Try it yourself! Relax your body and try to notice things around you with each of your senses.

Focused Meditation

Focused meditation is a little different to mindfulness meditation. In focused meditation, we try to focus our full attention on one thing.

Focusing on something for a long time can be more difficult than you may think!

Let's try it out! Get yourself a drink. Now, focus on it. Is it warm or cold? Can you smell it? What does it taste like? Every time your mind thinks about something else, return to your drink.

Guided Meditation

Guided meditation is led by someone who is not meditating. They might read from a script. They guide the person who is meditating through what to imagine and think about.

Let's try it. Ask a friend to close their eyes.

Then, read this script to them:

Breathe deeply. Imagine you are on a beach. Feel the warm water on your toes. Dig them into the cool sand. The Sun's heat feels warm on your skin. It helps your body relax.

Yoga Meditation

Yoga is an exercise for the body and the mind. When you practise yoga, you will make different shapes with your body while you focus on your breathing. The shapes are called poses. They all have special names.

Let's try Lotus pose! Follow these instructions.

1: Sit with your legs in front of you.

2: Cross your legs.

3: Bring your hands to your knees.

4: Close your eyes. Breathe deeply. Focus on every breath in and out.

Where Can I Meditate?

Now that you know all about meditation, it's time to find a place that works for you. You could find a quiet room at your home and take some time to practise.

If your home is noisy or isn't the right place for you, you could try to find a meditation class instead. Somebody will lead the class and guide you through how to meditate.

Looking After You

Meditation is a very good way to keep our minds healthy and calm. If meditation doesn't work for you, that's OK! There are lots of other ways to look after your mind.

Yoga and meditation go well together! Yoga can help you exercise both your body and mind. We have already tried Lotus pose, but there are so many more to try!

Mindfulness is another way to look after your mind. Being mindful means giving your full attention to something. If you are distracted when being mindful, notice the thought, but then return your attention to what you are doing.

The most important thing is making sure you do something to take care of yourself. It doesn't matter what it is.

Self-care is any activity you choose to do to look after your physical and mental health.

Index:

artists 12–13

breathing 22–23

classes 9, 25

homes 9, 24–25

India 8

senses 17, 19, 21

sportspeople 13

Meditation: Quiz

1. Do we know where or when meditation started?

2. Can you name a yoga pose?

3. Can you name a good thing that meditation can do for you?

4. Can you use the contents page to find information about mindfulness?

5. Using the index, can you find which page has information about India?

Helpful Hints for Reading at Home

This 'really readable' Accessible Reader has been carefully written and designed to help children with learning differences whether they are reading in the classroom or at home. However, there are some extra ways in which you can help your child at home.

- Try to provide a quiet space for your child to read, with as few distractions as possible.

- Try to allow your child as much time as they need to decode the letters and words on the page.

- Reading with a learning difference can be frustrating and difficult. Try to let your child take short, managed breaks between reading sessions if they begin to feel frustrated.

- Build your child's confidence with positive praise and encouragement throughout.

- Your child's teacher, as well as many charities, can provide you with lots of tips and techniques to help your child read at home.